OCEAN ANIMALS
— FROM —
HEAD TO TAIL

WRITTEN BY **Stacey Roderick**

ILLUSTRATED BY **Kwanchai Moriya**

Kids Can Press

What ocean animal has a head like this?

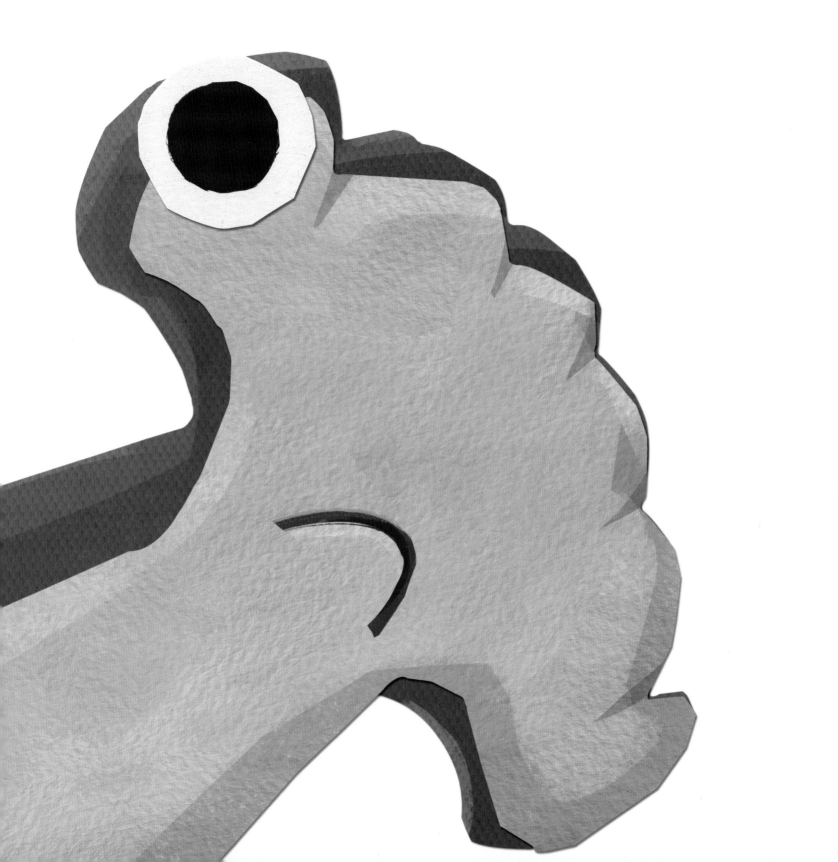

A hammerhead shark!

It's not hard to guess how *this* shark got its name. The fish's hammer-shaped head may look strange, but it's useful, too. The special shape means the shark's eyes are positioned to see above and below *at the same time!* This is particularly helpful when hunting for its favorite food — the stingray.

What ocean animal has eyes like this?

A colossal squid!

The colossal squid's soccer ball-sized eyes are the largest of any animal. The bigger an animal's eyes, the better it can see in areas where there is very little light. The squid's eyes are built for searching for prey (animals it eats) and watching out for predators (animals that eat it) in the deepest, darkest parts of the ocean.

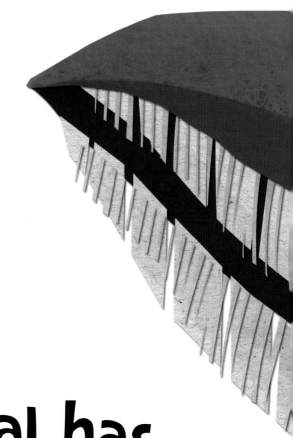

What ocean animal has a **mouth** like this?

A blue whale!

This huge animal — the biggest ever known — survives on tons of tiny shrimp-like creatures called krill. When the blue whale eats, it first swallows a mouthful of ocean water. Then, it lets the water flow back out through rows of baleen, the stiff bristles that grow down from the whale's top jaw. The baleen act like a giant sieve to catch all the tasty krill.

What ocean animal has a body like this?

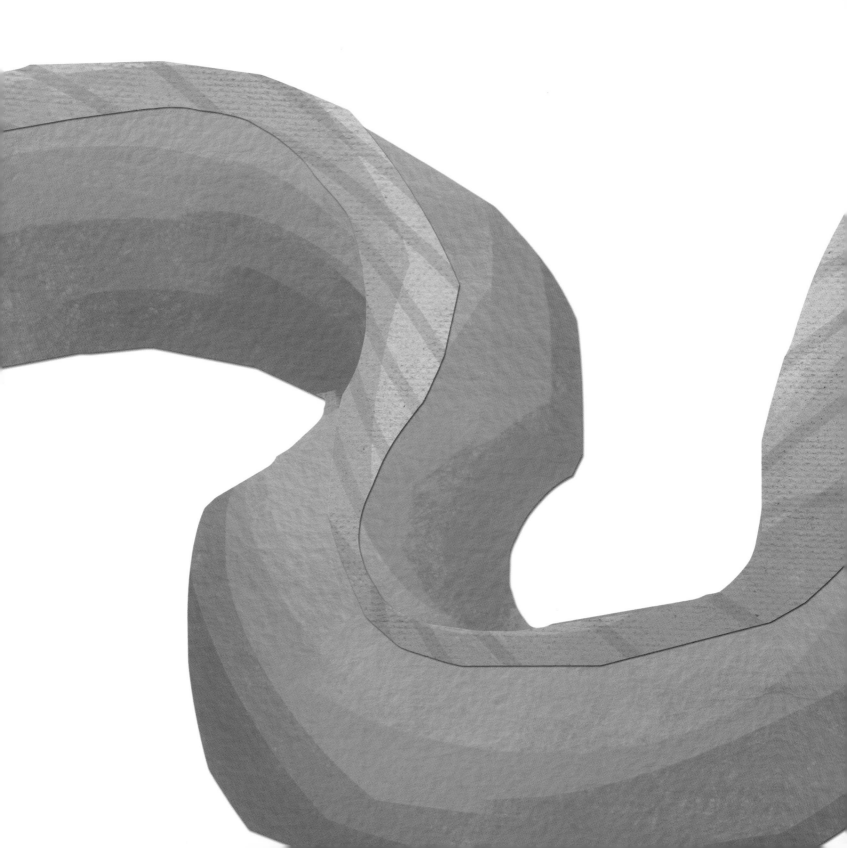

A moray eel!

The moray eel is actually a fish, even though it looks a lot like a snake as it slithers through the water. The eel's long, thin, muscular body easily bends and twists through coral reefs and into small rocky spaces. Here it can hide and wait for its next meal to pass by.

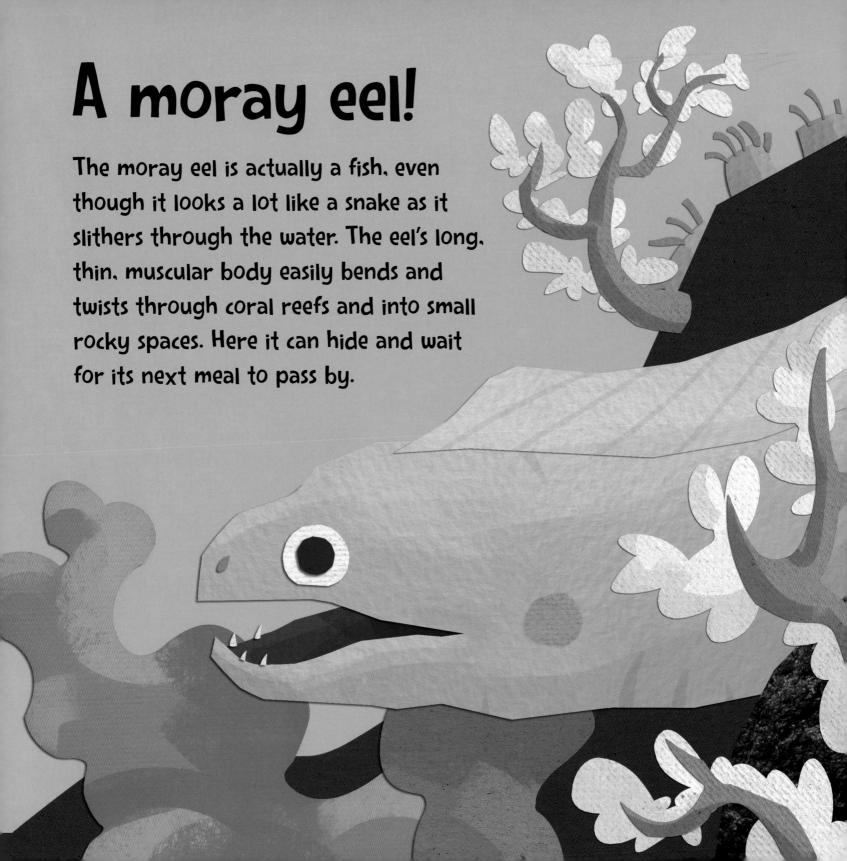

What ocean animal has a *fin* like this?

A sailfish!

Thought to be the fastest sea animal of all, the sailfish has a large fin running down its back. This fin can be raised and lowered, almost like the sail of a boat. But scientists aren't entirely sure what this fish uses its sail for. One idea is that it raises the sail when frightened to look bigger and fiercer, and scare off any possible threats.

What ocean animal has *flippers* like this?

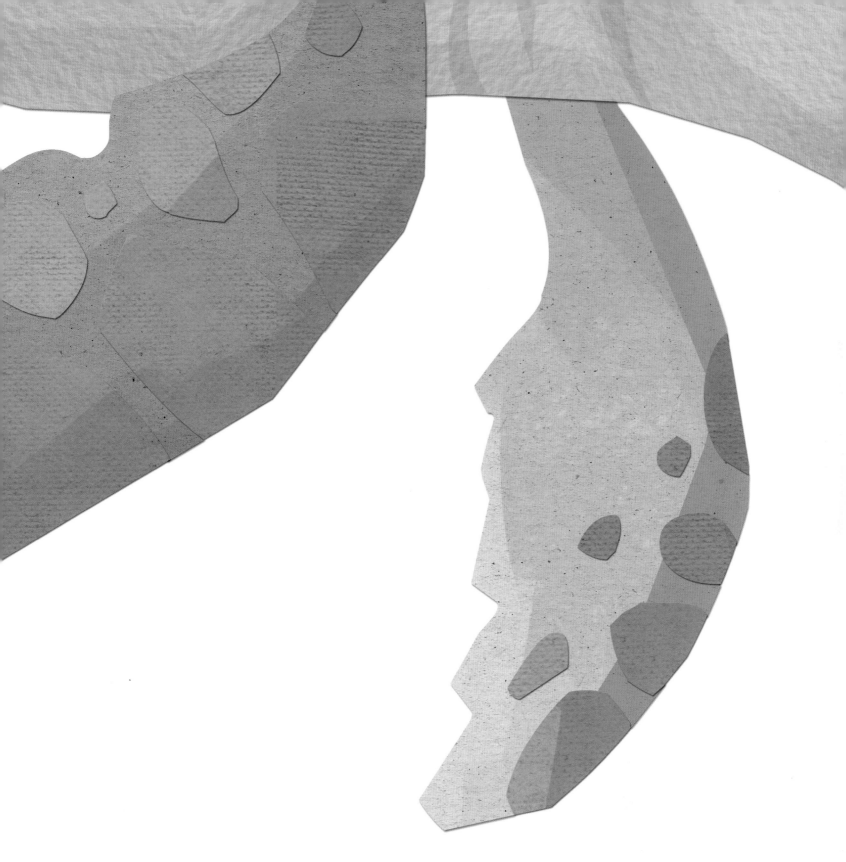

A green sea turtle!

Unlike their slow-moving cousins that live on land, green sea turtles are fast! These super swimmers use their flippers to zip through the water. The two front flippers act like paddles, powering the sea turtle forward. And the two back flippers are like the rudders of a boat, helping the turtle steer and keep steady.

What ocean animal has tentacles like this?

A sea anemone!

Although the colorful, tentacle-covered sea anemone (uh-NEM-uh-nee) looks more like a pretty flower than a hungry hunter, most fish don't want to get too close. That's because the sea anemone has tentacles filled with venom for stinging nearby prey. Once stung, the fish isn't able to move, and the anemone then uses its many tentacles to pull its dinner into its mouth.

What ocean animal has
a *tail* like this?

A seahorse!

Most fish use their tails for swimming and steering, but a seahorse uses its tail to get a grip! This small fish is not a strong swimmer, so it wraps its tail tightly around coral, sea grass and other weeds to keep from being swept away by ocean currents. A seahorse can also travel longer distances by attaching itself to floating seaweed and hanging on for the ride.

Other Awesome Ocean Animals

A trumpetfish is named for the shape of its long head and snout.

A starfish (or sea star) has an eye at the end of each of its arms.

The fangtooth's big mouth and spiky teeth have earned it another name — the ogrefish!

When in danger, the porcupinefish (or blowfish) puffs up its body like a spiky balloon.

A manatee uses its flippers for swimming and also to hold on to food and even other manatees.

An octopus actually has eight *arms*, not tentacles.

A stingray protects itself by whipping its tail around, which has spiny stingers.

A lionfish's spiny dorsal (back) fins are filled with a powerful venom.

For Owen and Brynn, cousins who get along swimmingly — S.R.
To One-Hyun, my fellow deep-sea adventurer, with love — K.M.

Acknowledgments
Many thanks to Dave Bader, Director of Education, Aquarium of the Pacific;
Stu Clausen, Assistant Curator, America's Wildlife Museum and Aquarium; and
Philip Willink, Senior Research Biologist, Shedd Aquarium, for generously sharing their time
and expertise to review this manuscript. And an ocean full of gratitude to my wonderful
KCP colleagues, with special thanks to Olga Kidisevic, Jennifer Grimbleby, DoEun Kwon,
Yvette Ghione, Genie MacLeod, Julia Naimska and Katie Scott.

Kids Can Press acknowledges the financial support of
the Government of Ontario, through the Ontario Media
Development Corporation's Ontario Book Initiative; the
Ontario Arts Council; the Canada Council for the Arts;
and the Government of Canada, through the CBF, for
our publishing activity.

Published in Canada by
Kids Can Press Ltd.
25 Dockside Drive
Toronto, ON M5A 0B5

Published in the U.S. by
Kids Can Press Ltd.
2250 Military Road
Tonawanda, NY 14150

www.kidscanpress.com

The artwork in this book was created in Adobe Photoshop
and Illustrator, using original photographs and textures.

The text is set in Squidtoonz.

Edited by Katie Scott
Designed by Julia Naimska

This book is smyth sewn casebound.
Manufactured in Shenzhen, China, in 3/2016 by Imago

CM 16 0 9 8 7 6 5 4 3 2 1

Library and Archives Canada Cataloguing in Publication

Roderick, Stacey, author
    Ocean animals from head to tail / written by Stacey
Roderick : illustrated by Kwanchai Moriya.

(Head to tail)
ISBN 978-1-77138-345-5 (bound)

    1. Marine animals — Juvenile literature. I. Moriya, Kwanchai,
illustrator II. Title.

QL122.2.R64 2016   j591.77   C2015-907233-6

Kids Can Press is a Corus™ Entertainment company